CREATIVITY

for
everybody

by
Kathryn P. Haydon
and
Jane Harvey

Printed in the United States of America

ISBN 978-0-9963856-9-5

Published by Sparkitivity, LLC
New York

Art and design by Jane Harvey
Photographs © Molly Gibbs (except p. 30)
Poems © Kathryn P. Haydon

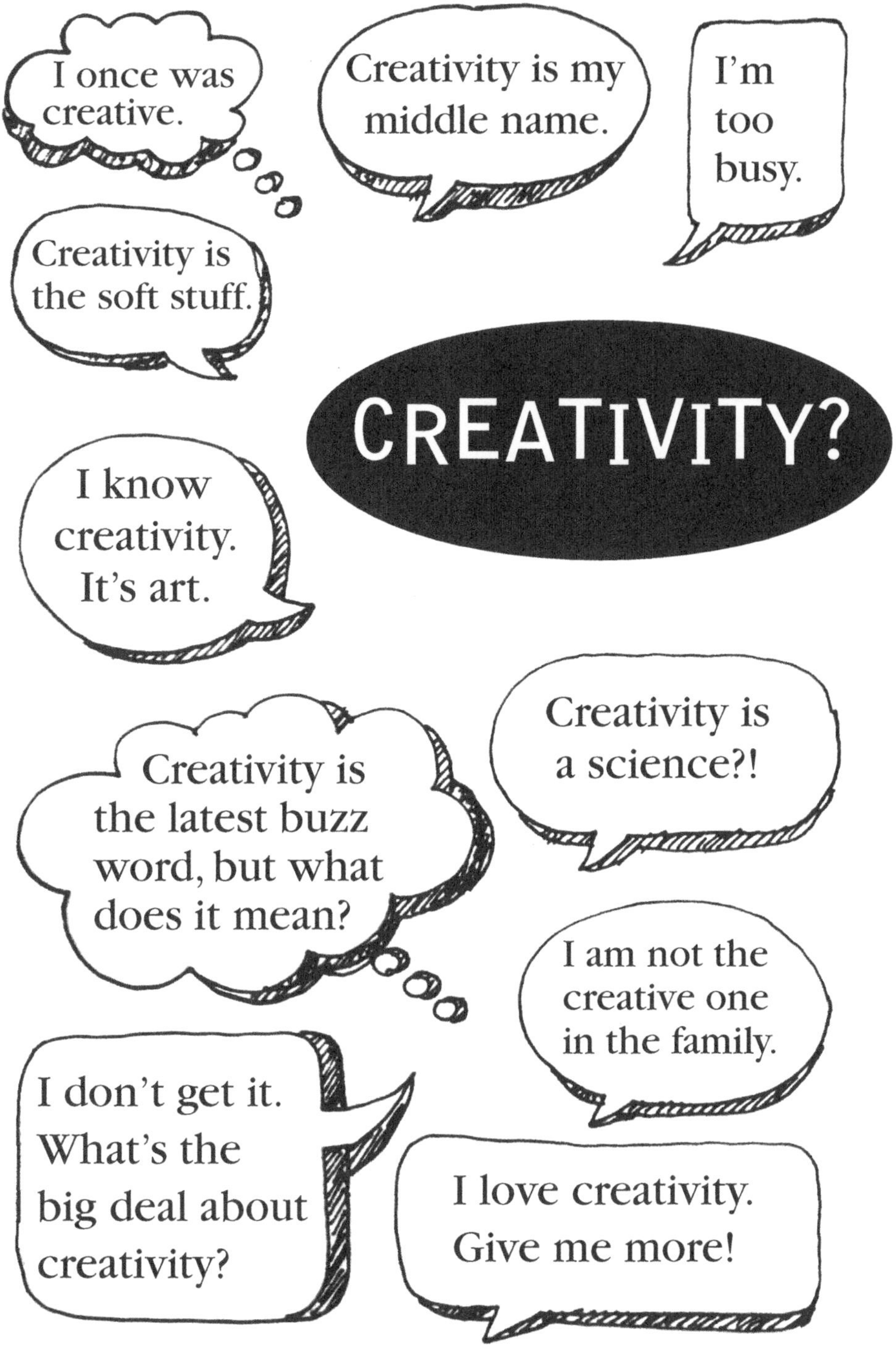
I once was creative.
Creativity is my middle name.
I'm too busy.
Creativity is the soft stuff.
CREATIVITY?
I know creativity. It's art.
Creativity is the latest buzz word, but what does it mean?
Creativity is a science?!
I am not the creative one in the family.
I don't get it. What's the big deal about creativity?
I love creativity. Give me more!

GRATITUDE

There are many people that supported this book-writing journey. Molly Gibbs, thank you for contributing your portfolio of photographs and for allowing us to share your talent. Katie Gibbs, thank you for your encouragement and joy. Jeff and C.J., we are grateful for your excitement, patience, and insightful feedback. Joan Franklin Smutny, you are a beacon of light, igniting creativity for children, teachers, and parents around the world; there are not words to thank you for what you have contributed. Dr. Cyndi Burnett, your enthusiasm and confidence in us was invaluable. We are grateful to The International Center for Studies in Creativity family, present and past, for carrying the torch that enables the academic study of creativity.

CREATIVITY for everybody

Creativity
is a word
so familiar
that you're sure
you know what
it means,
like that kid
whose hair is long
and streaked
purple
and you know
"his type,"
but when
you dig
a little deeper

you are
surprised
to find a
soul lined
with delicate gold.
Creativity
is the same.
You think
crafts or
woodworking
and then Monet
and Bach
like it's owned
by cliques

and the
typecast few;
a remote
aspiration
to plié in the
ballet
or become a
pop sensation
that's really a lie
you used
to tell if
they asked,
"what do you
want to be?"
But when you
dig deeper

you are
surprised
to find
an ever-
flowing
spring that is
your power
to think,
fresh waters
pouring forth
that feed the
winding stream.
You kneel down,
cup your hands,
take a long,
cool gulp —
resurgence;
it's yours,
and that's
creativity.

CONTENTS

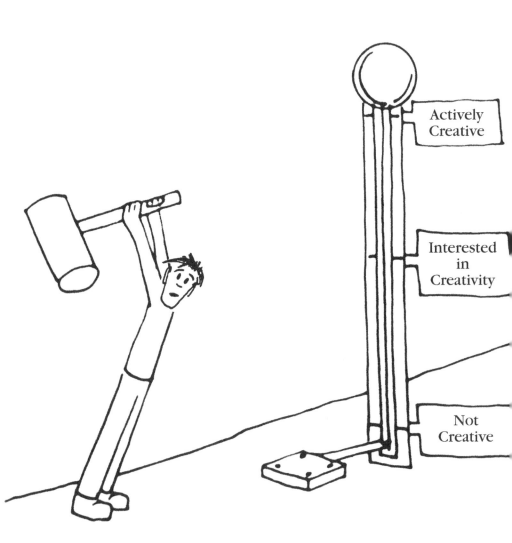

Actively
Creative

Interested
in
Creativity

Not
Creative

WHY CREATIVITY?

Do you realize that creativity is one of your prime superpowers? The simple awareness of what creativity actually means can be transformative. It can help you navigate obstacles, enhance your relationships, and connect you to your purpose, whether at home, work, or school.

With three-quarters of a century of empirical research, we know that creativity indeed belongs to everybody. Unfortunately, myths about creativity abound, and these misunderstandings hold us back as individuals and as a greater world community. This book provides a fast overview of what creativity entails. Whether you currently identify yourself as creative or not, you can use it for positive growth, change, and innovation.

If you hear yourself or others say, "I could never do that," try responding with, "What *can* you do?"

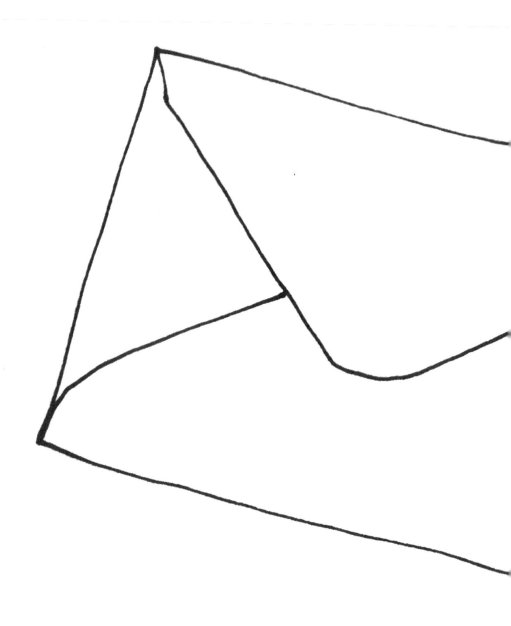

AN INVITATION

Learning about creativity should be a choose-your-own-adventure. That is why we have structured this book in two parts. The first section is designed to resonate with you personally and in small concept-bites, free of jargon from the academic field. We hope that you find it inspiring and engaging. The second section, "Dig Deeper," supports each page with notes and references from decades of research on the science of creativity.

We invite you to begin your excursion by reading this book in any way you choose: from cover to cover, flipping between the two sections, opening to a page now and again, or turning it sideways. This won't be the only book about creativity that you ever read, but we hope it empowers you to take hold of your own creative thinking and support the creativity of others around you.

Be curious,

Jane and Kathryn

If you read this book sideways, you'll find a flipbook of quick tips and reminders.

"Creativity is now as important in education as literacy..."

—Sir Ken Robinson

WHAT CREATIVITY IS NOT

Let's start with what creativity is *not*.

It is not owned by the arts, science, genius, or fame. It is not exclusive to folks like Mozart, Van Gogh, Edison, or Ella Fitzgerald.

In fact, everybody is creative.

We all use creativity in our everyday lives, all the time.

Children are creative. So are you, you just forgot. You don't have to be an artist to be creative.

MEMBERSHIP CARD
YOUR NAME
HERE_____
CREATIVITY

LOOKING

WHAT WE
DON'T SEE

500 DTL

ANGLES

FOCUS

FILTERS

SHADOWS

DISTANCE

SEEING

CREATIVITY IS SHIFTING PERSPECTIVE

Creativity requires new perspectives to break free of habits, assumptions, and automatic responses. Through active observing, noticing, finding patterns, sensing incongruencies, and making connections, our thoughts shift. Rethinking what we already know helps us gain new insights.

Creativity is the ability to think differently to tackle and overcome challenges. In order to get different, more favorable results, we must see anew. How do we attain another mode of thought to solve problems in new ways? That's what this book is about, but first we want to turn the focus to your inherent creative ability.

Try thinking like someone else: an alien, a rock, a stray cat, a high school math teacher.

creativity is

creativity is

creativity is

creativity is

thinking thinking is

thinking s

thinking

CREATIVITY IS THINKING

Have you improvised when you were trying to fix something? Have you figured out a way to stretch your dollars? Have you found an inventive new use for a flea market item? Have you thought of a way to explain a complex concept to a child?

In each case, you used your thinking to solve a problem in a way that was both valuable and original to you or someone else. That is creativity.

Cyndi's story on the next page illustrates that when either meaning or originality is absent, creativity is not being employed—even if you are involved in the arts.

You don't need to spend money on new supplies to learn to think creatively. All you need is your brain.

CREATIVITY ≠ THE ARTS

There is a general misunderstanding that creativity is only expressed in realms such as music, art, or theater. Cyndi experienced that the arts don't require creativity in every circumstance. A theater major fresh out of college, Cyndi moved to New York City. In her very first audition, she landed the role of the swing in *A Funny Thing Happened on the Way to the Forum* for the show's first national tour. She was ecstatic! Theater had been her main creative outlet all through school, and now she was living her dream. She used her creativity to learn her role, but too quickly faced a hard lesson. As she performed the show 189 times in 81 cities over six months, she realized that her job was to implement a role with practiced perfection. She felt like a cog in a wheel and her job required more conformity than original

thinking on her part. After that experience, Cyndi faced a personal crossroads and decided to pursue a career that would help her to more deeply understand and practice creative thinking. For her, it was important to discover that creative thinking fueled her drive more than perfomance.

Though creativity is not limited to the arts, the arts enhance creativity. Is there something you want to try?

permission

try

space

flexibility

time

choices

CREATIVITY IS FREEDOM

We *need* freedom in order to think creatively. The simple recognition that we each possess the ability to think for ourselves is the first step in claiming our own creative freedom.

Creativity *is* freedom, because it gives us new ideas and choices to solve problems. The more choices we have, the freer we are.

In essence, creativity is your power as an individual to think, learn, and grow.

"Everything that is really great and inspiring is created by the individual who can labor in freedom." —Einstein

Freedom

Webster says that liberty "is being free from restriction or control." I agree, of course, but add that freedom is knowing yourself.

You can't free yourself before you know yourself.

Before a baby bird knows it has wings it won't fly.

Newly aware the wings are there, he unfolds them, and has faith that they will sustain him as he soars.

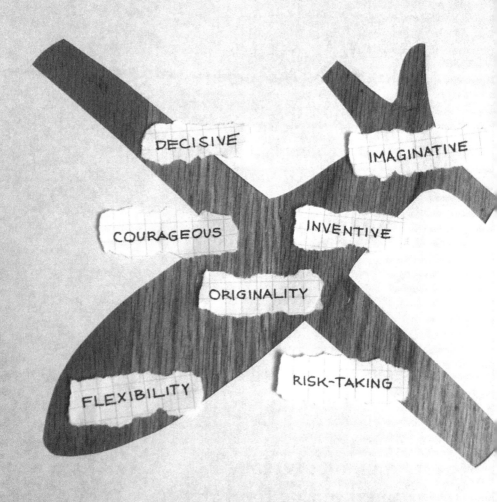

CREATIVITY IS ESSENTIAL

Creativity has always been essential to man's survival. Cultures, whether indigenous or modern, have used it to adapt to their changing environments over time. The connection between creativity and survival was noted by research in a 1950s study to understand why only a small number of fighter pilots were the most successful. Successful pilots employed the key characteristics of creative thinking, including imagination, inventiveness, originality, flexibility, courage, risk-taking, and quick decision-making. Creativity continues to be a matter of survival as we navigate a landscape of perpetually changing technology.

Sensible risk-taking should be encouraged. Playfulness and trust help when trying new things.

CREATIVITY IS PERSONAL

In order to survive and thrive, we need to start with what we have. Everyone has unique strengths to offer. We have these because we are human.

Your individuality is your power. But to use it, you have to know what it is. You have to know what lights you up.

When working with creativity, we always start from a standpoint of strengths. This may seem obvious, but we are living in a world that is constantly asking, "What is wrong with you and can it be fixed?"

Strengths give us leverage. If we don't first consider strengths, we have nothing to go on to tackle problems effectively. It's like trying to make a seesaw without a middle, a lever without a fulcrum.

Recognize the value of your individual uniqueness. Only you see and think as you do.

YOUR CREATIVITY

Let's zoom out and take an aerial view of you. You are a person with a unique makeup of strengths, values, motivations, and goals. Once you are aware of this, you can "use what you have to get what you want," to quote a friend.

People manifest creativity in different ways. Let's not ask, "Are you creative?" but instead ask, "In what ways are you creative?"

It starts from looking within. Have you ever identified your values, motivations, and goals?

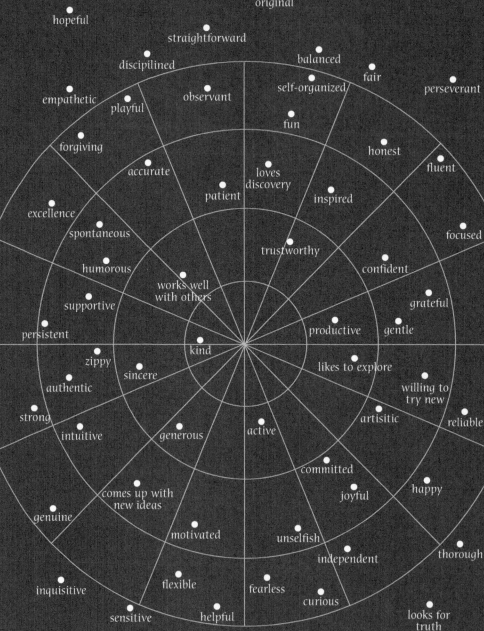

CHARACTERISTICS

Individual creativity is unique. Many of the qualities are part of all of us, but some shine brighter or flicker at different pulses.

Does the chart to the left remind you of the night sky? Imagine that each of the characteristics is a star, and identify which ones shine brightly for you. Consider as many as you wish, and imagine lines connecting, forming your own unique creative constellation. Think, too, about your children, employees, students, or new people you meet.

Being aware of creative constellations is a starting point to employ creativity and recognize it in others. Mandy's story on the next page explains how she leveraged her employees' strengths for an organizational turnaround.

Starburst Galaxy

You are
the night sky,
thick with
twinkling stars
clouding
the atmosphere.

My eyes adjust and
constellations leap
from the hazy luster,

tracing a path of
light points
that is your
power
to give.

27

LEVERAGING
STRENGTHS AT WORK

Mandy joined a firm of 45 people as the director of marketing. This family-owned company had a 30-year history, but the employees clearly were not working to their potential. The staff was uninspired, and not functioning as a team. They hadn't even held a team meeting in years! Mandy first met with individuals to determine their strengths, motivations, and goals; she reorganized the group based on these factors. Her boss was supportive and encouraged her decisions.

Now, the team is more productive, motivated, and accountable. They progress by learning together, celebrating successes publically, and finding training opportunities. Knowing everyone's long- and short-term goals, Mandy can assign special projects that align with skills and aspirations, instead

of basing them on proximity, friendship, reputation, or precedent. Regular weekly meetings are held to see the big picture, prioritize, and track success.

The energy and momentum of these changes have been tremendous. Job descriptions, motivation templates, and progress worksheets have been shared with other teams. Employees are happy, taking more initiative, and are talking about it. Teams have shifted into forward planning instead of reactive fire drills. People are more excited to come to work, and to focus on efforts that increase revenue for the firm. This workplace transformation began with a focus on individual strengths.

Find out what you love to do. What are all the ways you can incorporate it at home, work, or school?

PLAYFUL

OPEN

ASKS
QUESTIONS

IMAGINES

HUMOR

EXPLORES

OBSERVES

WONDERS

FRIENDS OF CURIOSITY

PRACTICING CREATIVITY

Like any skill, creativity can be developed and improved. Like everything, it takes practice. People who are regarded as highly creative practice these characteristics naturally. Think of Pelé and soccer. He may have begun with talent, but consider how many exercises, drills, and games led to his 1,281 career goals scored.

To practice creativity, you can start by exploring the creative characteristics. Curiosity is one easy entry point because it's an open doorway that leads directly to creative thinking. Everyone has a notion of what it means, and at least a distant memory from childhood. Curiosity involves a sense of wonder, exploration, searching, and inquiry. It supports lifelong learning and fresh inspiration.

From the photo, try on a different word each week. Keep track of what you do and reflect.

MISTAKES ARE OKAY

UNKNOWNS

POSSIBILITY

INTUITION

PERSPECTIVE

EXPLORE

NOVELTY

OPENNESS

One of the keys to practicing curiosity is openness. Openness requires exploring the unknown, not solving the problem right away, and being open to new ideas, possibilities, and change. It is suspending thoughts like "this will never work" until you have taken the time to generate and explore many new ideas.

Consider being open to the fact that you might not be right or that there is more than one way to do things. Maintaining an open mind leads to creative insights.

What are all of the ways you can get beyond your comfort zone and routine? (Hint: try something new.)

NEW **THINKING**

Question what we know well
Identify our assumptions.

Dig deeper
Ask questions that don't provide easy answers.

Open it up
Ask questions that invite new information.

Be a detective
Look for insights.

What if...?
Why?
How might...?

Reach further
Explore imaginative possibilitles.

INQUIRY

Being open to learning what we don't know paves the way for inquiry. As individuals, parents, workers, and teachers, we don't need to have all of the answers. Sometimes we learn more from not knowing the answer and engaging in discovery.

To do this, we have to be aware of how we ask questions. Common questions have available 'known' answers: "What is the current temperature?" or "What time is the meeting?" Questions like this don't require creativity. But, to engage people to participate and solve problems in surprising ways, we need to tweak our words and pose open-ended questions that invite new thinking.

Listen carefully to find questions that allow discovery for both asking and answering.

FINDING MEANING

Finding internal meaning is important for practicing creativity. It can relate to what you enjoy doing, personal connections, your mission, or a desire to give.

Going through the habitual motions of a repetitive task, such as packing school lunches, may start to become mindless. Connecting to an overall vision (like love for our children) might fuel us to do something meaningful (like write a special note or include a surprise food), which helps us find motivation.

Often we overlook an employee's or a child's need to find an individual identity, vision, or purpose within an organization or school. Bella's story on the next page shows how finding meaning can be life-changing.

Awareness of our vision or passion can help us get through the things we don't like doing.

MEANING SPARKS SUCCESS

When she was in third grade, Bella's teacher grew concerned. Bella's hand-writing was messy, her math facts were slow, and she was not engaged in class. Her parents became worried, but did not think there was something wrong with Bella. At home, they saw a curious, intrinsically motivated child who loved learning, especially about dinosaurs. Their intuition was that Bella's strengths and interests needed to be supported.

Bella loved science and began to attend after-school science classes, where she proved to be an engaged, productive student. Her parents continued to support her interest in being a paleontologist, and soon she was asked to create a hands-on class about dinosaurs for kindergarteners. Bella's teaching engaged the children in meaningful,

active learning for over an hour. She was in fifth grade. This experience catapulted her to starting her own business offering dinosaur classes to kids.

Now 13, she has worked in the dino lab at the Natural History Museum of Los Angeles, has won awards and scholarships for her experiments, and has been invited to meet leading scientists. Bella has worked hard in school and succeeded, fueled by the meaning she found in pursuing her passion, and her parents' dedication to advocating for her creativity.

Many kids like variety and may not have a focused interest. Let them explore and change interests.

CREATIVITY GETS EASIER

It isn't always easy to go against the grain and resist the typical lines of thinking. New and different thinking can cause discomfort to others. Since creativity sparks change, and people tend to feel uncomfortable about change, they often resist creativity.

Creativity requires commitment. It's sometimes uncomfortable to stand alone with an original idea, but it gets easier as we build confidence that our ideas are valuable. Courage, inner passion, vision, and purpose keep moving us forward. Learning from mistakes makes us stronger. Just think if the inventors and changemakers of the world had given up and blended in!

The 95th Floor

The elevator is
crowded with
SHOULDS.
Every button's lit up,
and more get on
at every floor,
shouting, whispering,
chattering, filling space
with expectations.

We reach the lobby
and they follow me
in a twisted conga line
through the
revolving door
and out onto the street.

I look up
and breathe deeply,
glad that the clouds
are walking through
the sky,
minding their own
business.

41

VISION PULLS US FORWARD

Like the lion in the *The Wizard of Oz*, Troy felt that he lacked courage. But once he learned about the power of creative thinking to build stronger teams that spur innovation, an inner drive was sparked. He became one of the most courageous first-level managers in a large, multi-billion dollar corporation.

What led Troy to overcome his intense feelings of vulnerability, fear, and insignificance to lead a creativity revolution inside his company? The typical biases against creative thinking were present as usual, but he was propelled by a strong, clear vision for company-wide collaboration and deliberate creativity. At times, outside resistance became so strong that he nearly gave up. But by tapping into

COURAGEOUS creativity

his vision, and staying connected to supportive allies, he was able to find his motivation even after frustrating setbacks.

Troy has made incredible progress working with internal teams on creative thinking and problem solving, leading to product innovations. Even better, he claimed and practiced the courageous creativity that he already had. By finding it, he and his colleagues have experienced the satisfaction and exhilaration of personal growth and transformation.

Creativity is not instant. It takes effort and time. Make the commitment to see it through.

ATTITUDES

PERCEPTIONS

MEANING

BEHAVIOR

BELIEFS

INFLUENCES

VALUES

ASSUMPTIONS

FEELINGS

ENVIRONMENT

MENTAL STATE

ECOSYSTEM

You don't live on an island. This is what makes creativity both a joy and a challenge. When you have the opportunity to collaborate creatively with people who value new thinking, it's fun. When the forces around you seem to work against you, it takes more persistence.

Your ecosystem involves the people you interact with, the way things get done, the culture, and the environment, both physical and mental. Oftentimes these components resist change, yet creativity causes change. What works well for one person may not be ideal for another. Being aware of both the positive and negative forces that affect creativity will help you to manage your ecosystem for successful creative growth.

Identify internal and external forces that hinder or fuel your ability to contribute original thinking.

POSITIVE ECOSYSTEMS

Robert has always lived and breathed creative characteristics, including original thinking and problem-solving ability. Back in his school years, he wasn't engaged and was not a star student. He was always working on new ideas in his head, and didn't see much of a point conforming to formal education methods. Therefore, he was not viewed as particularly bright by his teachers.

Robert comes from a family of small-town entrepreneurs, and he helped out in the family shop from an early age but was not burdened with the expectation to take it over. His parents allowed him to explore his own talents and interests, with a great deal of freedom. Robert's mother always saw his spark and supported his need to think independently and do things his own way. Although his school ecosystem didn't always work for him, his

family ecosystem was one of support:

- His parents clearly saw and valued his creative strengths.
- Family life was about pursuing individual growth, not following tradition.
- The physical space of the home was flexible and could be used for creative pursuits.
- The family valued and encouraged individual expression and progress.

Because of the support he received from his home ecosystem, Robert was able to fill his need for creative exploration outside of school through building projects, play, and business ventures. He went on to become a successful entrepreneur in his own right, continuing to channel his strengths to find and develop innovative solutions.

In what ways might you help to create a positive ecosystem for others in your life?

PEOPLE

People are part of our ecosystem, and oftentimes they can be biased against creativity. It has been shown that even people (bosses, teachers, parents) who say they value creativity actually react negatively to creative behavior and outcomes. Ironic, isn't it? Products and ideas that were born from creative thinking, and became essential to life, were almost always met with resistance when they were first introduced.

Naturally, individuals who bring new thinking might be perceived as challenging the established norms, and will face pressure to conform. As we begin to practice creative behavior and define ourselves by our creative characteristics, we grow into our unique strengths and the confidence to bravely express them.

Have you ever been resistant to a new product that you later adopted? Reflect on your change in thinking.

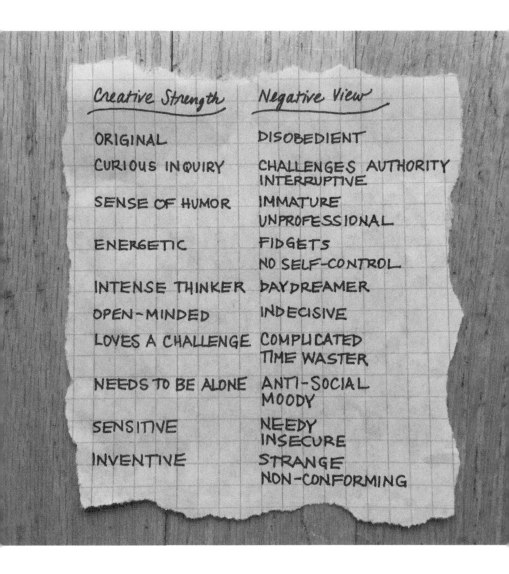

Creative Strength	Negative View
ORIGINAL	DISOBEDIENT
CURIOUS INQUIRY	CHALLENGES AUTHORITY INTERRUPTIVE
SENSE OF HUMOR	IMMATURE UNPROFESSIONAL
ENERGETIC	FIDGETS NO SELF-CONTROL
INTENSE THINKER	DAYDREAMER
OPEN-MINDED	INDECISIVE
LOVES A CHALLENGE	COMPLICATED TIME WASTER
NEEDS TO BE ALONE	ANTI-SOCIAL MOODY
SENSITIVE	NEEDY INSECURE
INVENTIVE	STRANGE NON-CONFORMING

STRENGTHS MISLABELED

Sometimes we have to overcome misinterpretation of our creative strengths. For example, your inclination to ask questions to get to the bottom of things might seem like you are always challenging authority. Or, your desire to tackle difficult and ill-defined problems might make doing rote work so painful that you leave bills unpaid or math homework undone. Your sensitivity and intuition might make it unbearable to be in an environment where a boss or a teacher doesn't treat you with respect. If we can identify where creative behaviors are misinterpreted, we can learn how to more effectively take responsibility and employ these characteristics as productive strengths.

Radiance

You're a beautiful shadow,
they say,

dark cast of a tree,
branches and stems
spread regally upon
the snow

and particularly stunning
on this perfectly
moonlit night.

But they don't understand.

I am a warm sun ray
that the moon reflects
and the tree blocks
to create
the elegant shadow
by night and by day,
I warm the earth
I melt the snow

I am not the shadow,
I am light.

IDEAS

Ideas are infinite, and new ideas are needed for change, progress, and growth. There is an invisible snowstorm of ideas all around us all the time. Ideas come from our unique thinking and experiences that we connect and intersect.

Ideas are not solutions, and they are not opinions. They are sometimes tiny and fragile, or wacky and immense. Ideas can arise from a moment of clarity, or from observation, steady work, collaborative experiences, restful moments, or escape time like a walk in nature.

It takes practice to come up with ideas, and the more we practice, record our ideas, and go beyond the obvious, the more fluent we become.

What problem are you working on? Challenge yourself to come up with 30 ideas to solve it.

EXPRESSION

When a new idea, born in the imagination, is expressed, it can be defined as creative because then it has the potential to become useful or meaningful. Creative thinking is active, and results in change. Much creativity emerges from collaboration and building on other's ideas.

Ideas need to be expressed. Many people keep a notebook to capture ideas before they are forgotten. This is a way to practice and value original thinking. And who knows? One of your ideas, scribbled on a page in the middle of the night, might contribute to positive change.

Take responsibility for your ideas. Value them. Write them down and make them happen.

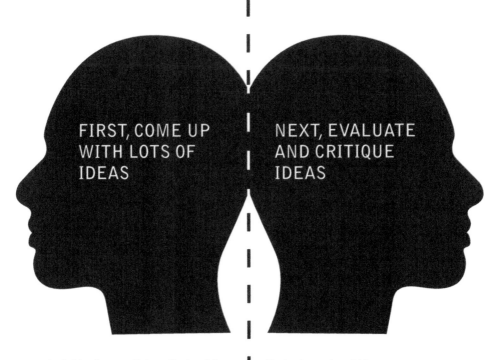

FIRST, COME UP WITH LOTS OF IDEAS

NEXT, EVALUATE AND CRITIQUE IDEAS

Individually or collaboratively, strive to come up with ideas, and then more . . .

Evaluate and sort ideas.

Go ahead and allow the novel and crazy ones. They can lead to innovation.

Check that your ideas are on track with your goals.

Individually or collaboratively, build from ideas to make new ones.

Ideas are valuable. Try to find something good in several ideas.

Wait to judge or evaluate any of the ideas. There is time for that later. Give them a chance to exist first.

Ideas can always be improved upon. Don't assume that the best ideas are immediate.

CARING FOR IDEAS

In the creative process, there are two distinct mental actions that serve ideas: generating multiple ideas, then evaluating those ideas to choose which make the most sense under the circumstances. It is essential that these two actions are given their own space and time.

Give yourself time to dream. At school, this might mean taking a few minutes to write down all the possible topics for your essay, and then choosing the best one for the assignment. In a business meeting, take the time to first come up with ideas to solve a challenge and wait to evaluate them until many options have been put forth.

Separate idea generating from idea choosing. This is a key to high-level creative thinking.

JUDGING IDEAS

If we really want new and improved
solutions that lead to innovation,
evaluation of ideas must be done
with care. Training ourselves to look
beyond our first reactions supports
ongoing creativity and helps us find
seeds that can be developed further.

Even if we tend to immediately
see flaws, we can deliberately
flip our thinking and commit to
finding a positive. Try leading with:
"One thing I like about this idea is
_____." This even works
when you are evaluating your
own ideas. Practicing affirmative
judgment holds the door open to
new possibilities.

Practice eliminating "No." Try saying, "Yes, and..." in your response to others, especially when you don't agree.

treat other
people's
creativity

the way you
would like them
to treat yours

THE GOLDEN RULE OF CREATIVITY

COLLABORATION

When you recognize your own creative strengths, and practice the golden rule of creativity, you create a solid foundation for creative growth. It's important to leave space for creativity in yourself and others, to be open to it and allow it. As you pursue your own thoughts and ideas, connect with others when your motivations overlap. If we are each practicing our own creativity, and supporting those around us by honoring their creativity as well, we strengthen and inspire each other. In the creative process, there is time and space for independent thought as well as collaboration. Sometimes it's a matter of preference, and sometimes necessity, but both are valid and useful.

Concentric

All this time
I thought that
we are circles
spinning through
the cosmos
in our orbits,
every now and then
eclipsing,
while moving along
our paths.
But then you told me
we are color,
each of us
a separate hue,
all needed,
all good.
I looked again
and squinted
and we blended –
gleaming.
You taught me
that together
we are one.

'PROCESS'
MEANS
ACTION

62

PROCESS

The best way to get started with creativity is to jump in:

- Actively search and explore without expectations.
- Be receptive.
- Welcome challenge and be open to what you discover along the way.
- Dedicate time and effort.
- Experiment, adapt, adjust, learn.
- Be confident and don't give up.

Solutions come from the interconnection of knowledge, experience, imagination, attitude, and finally, how we evaluate what we come up with. Though there are many tools and processes available to help, there is no one right way and you have to find what works for you. Remember, we all use creativity in our everyday lives all the time; build on what you already do.

Start noticing how you approach solving problems creatively and when you feel the most fluent.

TIME FOR IDEAS
DYNAMISM/ LIVELINESS
SUPPORT FOR IDEAS
DEBATE
FREEDOM
TRUST/ OPENNESS
PLAYFULNESS/ HUMOR
RISK-TAKING
TENSION/ CONFLICT
CHALLENGE

ENVIRONMENT

We said earlier that freedom is essential for creative thinking, and this has a lot to do with a person's physical and mental environment. Whether in a school, family, or business, there's a balance that must be struck to allow for the right amount of freedom to explore one's own ideas. This might be accommodated by the culture—how things get done, how people are treated— or by the physical space. It's about giving ourselves and others the opportunity to play with ideas and think freely, whether collaboratively or individually. A climate of trust and support enables confidence and the courage to take creative risks.

Ask around. What are people's ideal creative environments, both mental and physical?

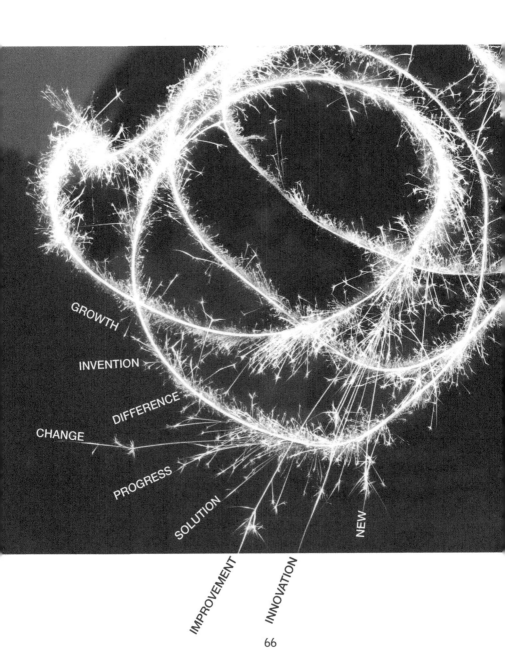

GROWTH

INVENTION

DIFFERENCE

CHANGE

PROGRESS

SOLUTION

NEW

IMPROVEMENT

INNOVATION

OUTCOME

Creativity doesn't always yield world-changing inventions, but it invariably sparks some form of change once that new thinking is applied. The outcome might be a meaningful personal realization, a different approach to parenting, a unique solution for a community issue, or a new service offering at work. Whether the scale is large or small, the outcome of creative thinking leads to innovation, social change, and personal progress.

We don't always have to react to change. We can create it. Look for the ideas behind change. Move forward, and create some sparks.

What might be all the ways your thoughts can make a difference? Notice how your ideas ignite change.

GOING BEYOND

Creativity doesn't happen overnight, but awareness—thinking about your thinking and the potential of your creativity—can expand your perspective and open up possibilities. It is not magic, but it can feel magical once you start practicing creative thinking and noticing it in others.

Now it's time to ask again: Do you consider yourself creative? We hope that you go beyond "yes," and now have several ideas to respond when asking yourself the question, "In what ways am I creative?"

With new thinking, you can go beyond where you have been before. (A nod to E. Paul Torrance.)

DIG DEEPER

The following is a collection of endnotes as academic support for each page of the book. Because the research on creativity continues to grow, our intent is to provide the origin of each concept or refer to a scholar who has studied that area in depth. These roots support the foundational base of the field of creativity. If you are interested in learning more, this is a great place to sample some of the research.

6–7 WHY CREATIVITY?

Ruth Richards coined the term "everyday creativity" (Richards, Kinney, Benet, & Merzel, 1988) and has written widely on the topic: "The construct of everyday creativity is defined in terms of human originality at work and leisure across the diverse activities of everyday life. It is seen as central to human survival, and to some extent, it is (and must be) found in everyone" (Richards, 2010, p. 190).

Richards, R. (2010). Everyday creativity. In Kaufman, J. C., & Sternberg, R. J., (Eds.), *The Cambridge handbook of creativity* (pp. 189-215). New York, NY: Cambridge University Press.

Richards, R., Kinney, D. K., Benet, M., & Merzel, A. P. (1988). Assessing everyday creativity: Characteristics of the Lifetime Creativity Scales and validation with three large samples. *Journal of Personality and Social Psychology*, 54(3), 476-485.

10–11 WHAT CREATIVITY IS NOT

The science of creativity has been researched and studied empirically for decades. Academic fieldwork was spurred by a seminal speech given by J. P. Guilford to the American Psychological Association in 1950. Substantial research continued in the 1950s and 1960s, when the Soviet launching of Sputnik fueled a national drive for innovation in the United States. Guilford and early researchers demonstrated that creativity is a different form of intelligence, not necessarily measured by IQ tests, and that all people are capable of creative acts. Wrote Guilford, "Creative acts can therefore be expected, no matter how feeble or how infrequent, of almost all individuals. The important consideration here is the concept of continuity. Whatever the nature of creative talent may be, those persons who are recognized as creative merely have more of what all of us have" (Guilford, 1950, p. 446).

Guilford, J.P. (1987). The 1950 presidential address to the American Psychological Association. In S. G. Isaksen (Ed.) *Frontiers of creativity research: Beyond the basics* (pp. 33-45). Buffalo, NY: Bearly Limited.

Guilford, J. P. (1950). Creativity. *American Psychologist*, 5, 444-454.

Robinson, K. (February 2006). Ken Robinson: *How schools kill creativity* [Video file]. Retrieved from http://www.ted.com/talks/ken_robinson_says_schools_kill_creativity

Unesco Institute for Statistics. (2014, September) UIS fact sheet. Retrieved from http://www.uis.unesco.org/literacy/Documents/fs-29-2014-literacy-en.pdf

12–13 CREATIVITY IS SHIFTING PERSPECTIVE

E. Paul Torrance defined creativity as "the process of sensing difficulties, problems, gaps in information, missing elements, something askew: making guesses and formulating hypotheses about these deficiencies; evaluating and testing these guesses and hypotheses; possibly revising and retesting them and finally communicating the results" (Torrance, 1988, p. 47). Looking at creativity as a problem solving process, as Torrance defined it, gives us another way to see that everybody is creative.

Torrance, E. P. (1969). *Creativity*. San Rafael, CA: Dimensions Publishing Company.
Torrance, E. P. (1988). The nature of creativity as manifest in its testing. In R.G. Sternberg (Ed.), *The nature of creativity: Contemporary perspectives*. New York, NY: Cambridge University Press.

14–15 CREATIVITY IS THINKING

creativity is thinking

The most well-known definition of creativity focuses on two qualifiers: novelty and usefulness. This wording was first put forth by Mo Stein in 1953: "The creative work is a novel work that is accepted as tenable or useful or satisfying by a group at some point in time . . ." (p. 311). Who defines originality and usefulness? Stein said that both internal and external measures must be considered. Therefore, creativity can be judged as useful on a personal level, or on a societal level. Recently, some scholars have substituted the word "valuable" for "useful" when defining creativity (Puccio, Reisman, & Matson, 2014).

Puccio, G. J., Reisman, F., & Matson, J. V. (Panel). (2014, September 11). *Teaching creativity* [Radio broadcast]. In Marty Moss-Coane (Producer), Philadelphia, PA: National Public Radio. Retrieved from http://whyy.org/cms/radiotimes/2014/09/11/teaching-creativity/
Runco, M. A., & Jaeger, G. J. (2012). The standard definition of creativity. *Creativity Research Journal*, 24(1), 92-96.
Stein, M. I. (1953). Creativity and culture. *Journal of Psychology*, (36), 311-322.

16–17 CREATIVITY ≠ THE ARTS

Mark Runco wrote that there is an "art bias" that limits our understanding of creativity. His research has shown that parents and teachers tend to hold mistaken beliefs, such as thinking that all creative children are artistic. Runco cautioned that it is important to know that creativity crosses all disciplines; if we limit it to the context of art, we will miss out on developing creative potential in a wider population of individuals (Runco, 2007).

Runco, M. A. (2007). *Creativity: Theories and themes: Research, development, and practice*. Detroit, MI: Thomson Gale.

18–19 CREATIVITY IS FREEDOM

Einstein often referred to the power of individual thinking, and this can be seen in the context of his well-known statement: ". . . [E]very individual should have the opportunity to develop the gifts which may be latent in him. Alone in that way can the individual obtain the satisfaction to which he is justly entitled; and alone in that way can the community achieve its richest flowering. For everything that is really great and inspiring is created by the individual who can labour in freedom" (Einstein, 1950, p. 19).

Beginning in the 1970s, Teresa Amabile has researched motivations behind creativity. She concluded that intrinsic (versus extrinsic) motivation is essential for creativity. Her work draws from that of Carl Rogers (1954), who maintained that freedom to internally regulate creative pursuits is essential to creativity. Amabile (1998) named freedom as one of the ideal conditions to support creativity in the workplace.

Amabile, T. (September, 1998). How to kill creativity. *Harvard Business Review*. Retrieved from https://hbr.org/1998/09/how-to-kill-creativity/ar/1

Einstein, A. (1950). *Out of my later years*. New York, NY: Citadel Press.

Ekvall, G. (1983). Climate, structure and innovativeness in organizations: A theoretical framework and an experiment. *Report 1*. Stockholm: FAradet.

Rogers, C. (1954). Towards a theory of creativity. *ETC: A Review of General Semantics* 11, 249-260.

20–21 CREATIVITY IS ESSENTIAL

Torrance and colleagues (Torrance, Rush, Kohn, & Doughty, 1957) conducted the fighter pilot study for the Air Force Survival School in the 1950s. Reflecting on that experience, Torrance (2003) wrote, "I found my first, and in many ways the best, definition of 'creativity' there. At the Survival School, air crews were trained to survive in emergency and extreme conditions for which they had no learned and practiced behavior... In the fighter interceptor pilot study, I met the most creative group of men I have ever encountered" (p. 53). One of the conclusions that Torrance made from this study was that creative problem solving should be a part of survival training (Torrance, 1984).

Torrance, E. P. (1984). The role of creativity in identification of the gifted and talented. *Gifted Child Quarterly*, 28(4), 153-156.

Torrance, E. P. (2003). The millenium: A time for looking forward and looking back. *Illinois Association for Gifted Children Journal*, 53-59.

Torrance, E. P., Rush, Jr., C.H., Kohn, H. B., & Doughty, J. M. (1957). *Factors in fighter-interceptor pilot combat effectiveness*. Lackland Air Force Base, TX: Air Research and Development Command.

22–23 CREATIVITY IS PERSONAL

The man who appealed for the scientific study of creativity back in 1950, J. P. Guilford (1977), stated, "Knowing the nature of your abilities, you will be able to turn them on when you need them and you will learn how to exercise them in order to strengthen them" (p. 12). This underscores the point that awareness and identification of strengths is important. Appreciative Inquiry is one method that builds from strengths to catalyze change. It was originally developed as a business change management process and can be applied to many problem solving situations. (Whitney & Cooperrider, 2005).

Guilford, J. P. (1977). *Way beyond the IQ: Guide to improving intelligence and creativity*. Buffalo, NY: Creative Education Foundation.

Whitney, D., & Cooperrider, D. L. (2005). *Appreciative Inquiry: A positive revolution in change*. San Francisco, CA: Berrett-Koehler Publishers.

24–25 YOUR CREATIVITY

Feldhusen and Hobson (1972) noted, "Research on creativity has stressed creative behavior as a cognitive function. Little attention has been paid to affect—to feelings and emotions. Work by Torrance, Wallach and Kogan, and Getzels and Jackson suggests, however, that creative thinking is more than cognition. Creative thinking also involves feelings, emotions, attitudes, and values. Programs to encourage creative thinking should develop these affective components" (p. 148). There are three fundamental skills/dispositions/attitudes that are essential to creativity: openness to novelty, tolerance for ambiguity, and tolerance for complexity. These three undergird key affective skills found in each stage of creative problem solving: "mindfulness, dreaming, sensing gaps, playfulness, avoiding premature closure, sensitivity to environment, and tolerance for risks" (Puccio, Mance, & Murdock, 2011, p. 73).

Feldhusen, J. F., & Hobson, S. K. (1972). Freedom and play: Catalysts for creativity. *The Elementary School Journal*, 73(3), 148-155.
Puccio, G. J., Mance, M., & Murdock, M. C. (2011). *Creative leadership: Skills that drive change*. (2nd ed). Thousand Oaks, CA: Sage Publications.

26–27 CHARACTERISTICS

Studies about eminent creators help us to recognize creative behaviors in ourselves so that we can practice them to strengthen our creativity. Mackinnon (1962) was a pioneer in creativity research whose motive was to better understand creative characteristics so that these could be supported and nurtured early in people's lives.

Davis (2004) conducted a comprehensive literature review, sorting hundreds of adjectives and descriptions of creative personality traits into sixteen main categories: aware of creativeness, original, independent, risk-taking, high energy, curious, sense of humor, capacity for fantasy, attracted to complexity or ambiguity, artistic, open-minded, thorough, needs alone time, perceptive, emotional, and ethical (p. 84). Not everyone manifests all of the categories, but these groupings do synthesize recurring characteristics of creative people.

Davis, G. (2004). *Creativity is forever*. Dubuque, IA: Kendall-Hunt.
Mackinnon, D. W. (1962). The nature and nurture of creative talent. *The American Psychologist*, 17(7), 484-495.

28–29 LEVERAGING STRENGTHS AT WORK

Teresa Amabile has conducted significant research regarding the conditions that support positive employee emotions, motivations, and attitudes. Amabile and Kramer (2011) found that the most important factor is "making progress in meaningful work" (p. 77). What they call the "progress principle" has to do with small wins. Amabile and Kramer's work has shown that the more small wins people experience, the greater their creative productivity.

Amabile, T., & Kramer, S. (2011). *The progress principle*. Boston, MA: Harvard Business Review Press.

30–31 PRACTICING CREATIVITY

A recent meta-analytic study by Scott, Leritz, & Mumford (2004) found that well-designed creativity training programs led to increased creative output. The Creative Studies Project reported decades of research that showed that creativity can be developed when it is deliberately nurtured (Parnes, 1987).

Many researchers have maintained that curiosity sparks creativity. One of the pioneers in curiosity research, Daniel E. Berlyne (1960), divided curiosity into four categories: 1). the desire to know 2). the desire to try, experience, and feel 3). seeking novelty and challenge 4). investigating uncertainty or complexity. You will recognize in these categories elements that underlie creativity. A significant force behind academic achievement and invention is intellectual curiosity (Harvey, 2015; Von Stumm, Hell, & Chamorro-Premuzic, 2011).

Berlyne, D. E. (1960). *Conflict, arousal, and curiosity*. New York, NY: McGraw-Hill.
Harvey, J. (2015). Is curiosity a first step to explain creativity? In Culpepper, M. K., & Burnett, C. (Eds.), *Big questions in creativity* 2015. Buffalo, NY: ICSC Press.
Parnes, S. (1987). The creative studies project. In Isaksen, S. (Ed.), *Frontiers of creativity research: Beyond the basics* (pp. 156-188). Buffalo, NY: Bearly Limited.
Scott, G. M., Leritz, L. E., & Mumford, M. D. (2004). The effectiveness of creativity training: A meta-analysis. *Creativity Research Journal*, 16, 361-388.
Von Stumm, S., Hell, B., & Chamorro-Premuzic, T. (2011). The hungry mind: Intellectual curiosity is the third pillar of academic performance. *Perspectives on Psychological Science*, 6(6), 574-588.

32–33 OPENNESS

Ruth Noller's definition of creativity shows that knowledge, imagination, and evaluation can't escape the positive effects of a receptive attitude, which begins with a posture of openness. Noller's formula is C = f_a(K, I, E), or, "Creativity is a function of Knowledge, Imagination, and Evaluation, reflecting an

$$C = f_a(K, I, E)$$

interpersonal attitude toward the beneficial and positive use of creativity" (Isaksen, Dorval, & Treffinger, 2010, p. 5; Noller, 2001).

Isaksen, S. G., Dorval, B. K., & Treffinger, D. J. (2010). *Creative approaches to problem solving: A framework for innovation and change* (3rd ed.). Thousand Oaks, CA: Sage.
Noller, R. B. (2001). Dr. Ruth B. Noller: Contributions to Creativity. ICSC Founder Talks. [Video file]. Buffalo, NY.

34–35 INQUIRY

Jacob Getzels termed inquiry as "problem finding" (Getzels, 1982; Getzels & Csikszentmihalyi, 1976). He believed that the most important element for creativity was defining a problem by asking the right questions. Sidney Parnes, another pioneer in applied creativity, also maintained that proper wording of a challenge question is essential. He suggested beginning with "How might . . .?" to formulate open-ended challenge questions (Parnes, 1967, p. 125). More recently, Anna Craft (2000) defined "possibility thinking" and called it the "engine" of creativity. A question that is "possibility broad" is akin to a "What if . . .?" question, and she believed it important to pose these questions to students while giving them plenty of freedom and time to explore (Chappell, Craft, Burnard, & Cremin, 2008).

Getzels, J. W. (1982). The problem of the problem. In R. Hogarth (Ed.), *New directions for methodology of social and behavioral science: Question framing and response consistency* (pp. 37- 49). San Francisco: Jossey-Bass.

Getzels, J.W. & Csikszentmihalyi, M. (1976). *The creative vision: A longitudinal study of problem finding in art.* New York, NY: John Wiley & Sons, Inc.

Parnes, S. J. (1967). *Creative behavior guidebook.* New York, NY: Scribner.

Chappell, K., Craft, A., Burnard, P., & Cremin, T. (2008). Question-posing and question-responding: The heart of 'Possibility Thinking' in the early years. *Early Years: An International Journal of Research and Development*, 28(3), pp. 267-286.

Craft, A. (2000) *Creativity across the primary curriculum: Framing and developing practice.* London: RoutledgeFalmer.

36–37 FINDING MEANING

When we have purpose and meaning, we are able to make a connection to something greater than ourselves but not necessarily outside of ourselves. Experienced creators, such as Einstein, often relied on intuition as a guide. He stated, "To [some] elementary laws there leads no logical path, but only intuition, supported by being sympathetically in touch with experience" (Holton, 1988, p. 375).

Holton, G. J. (1988). *Thematic origins of scientific thought: Kepler to Einstein.* Boston, MA: Harvard University Press.

38–39 MEANING SPARKS SUCCESS

Torrance and Safter (1999) wrote about teachers who applied "second-order change solutions" to help students overcome reading challenges: "The teachers did not make a direct attack on the reading . . ." (p. 6). Typical solutions like reading interventions had already been tried, to no avail. The teachers who ultimately helped the children worked from a standpoint of strengths. They were able to dig deeper to find the real issue, try a totally different solution, and more than reading success was realized: behaviors and attitudes changed and students were more engaged and successful.

In summary, there are three main guidelines that help with developing second-order change solutions: 1). look outside of the problem situation, or reframe it 2). reword the question, such as, "What might be all of the ways to inspire this student to engage with words?" 3). get away from "more of the same" and try something entirely new (Torrance & Safter, 1999, p. 8). The fundamental principle behind second-order change solutions is connecting students with meaning.

Torrance, E. P. & Safter, H. (1999). *Making the creative leap beyond. . .* Amherst, MA: Creative Education Foundation Press.

40–41 CREATIVITY GETS EASIER

Kaufman and Beghetto developed the Four C Model of Creativity to support the fact that though everyone is creative, not all creativity is on the same scale. They defined the following four categories of creativity: *mini-c*: personal aspects of creativity, transformational learning, creative insights; *little-c*: daily innovations by non-experts; *Pro-c*: professional expertise but not at the eminent level; *Big-C*: eminent contributions on a societal level, as validated by history (Kaufman & Beghetto, 2009).

Learning from well-known individuals about their creative characteristics can help support our own efforts and inspire us to persevere. Traits that are common among eminent creators are vision, courage, independence, and resilience. There are other examples, but Smutny and von Fremd (2014) did a particularly good job highlighting the importance of these characteristics in a selection of vignettes about famous women.

Kaufman, J. C., & Beghetto, R. A. (2009). Beyond big and little: The Four C Model of Creativity. *Review of General Psychology*, 13(1), 1-12.
Smutny, J. F., & von Fremd, S. E. (2014). *The lives of great women leaders and you*. Unionville, NY: Royal Fireworks Press.

42–43 VISION PULLS US FORWARD

Torrance (1987) reported on his longitudinal study that has now continued for over 50 years. It demonstrated that people's vision for their future was a significant predictor of creative achievement. Visionary thinking is an essential component of creativity. The dreaming state puts us in a mindset to achieve what we imagine, and it pulls us through present obstacles. Vision allows us to discover meaning, purpose, opportunity, potential, and inspiration. Beginning with phrases like, "Wouldn't it be great if . . .?" can start us on the road to visioning (Puccio, Mance, & Murdock, 2011).

Puccio, G. J., Mance, M., & Murdock, M. (2011). *Creative leadership: Skills that drive change*. [2nd ed.].. Thousand Oaks, CA: Sage Publications.
Torrance, E. P. (1987). Future career image as a predictor of creative achievement in a 22-year longitudinal study. *Psychological Reports* (60), 2, 574-574.

44–45 ECOSYSTEM

In 1961, Mel Rhodes introduced the idea of creativity as a system made up of several components: person (who), process (how), press/ environment (where), and product (outcome). Each of these aspects plays upon the others as they form a system that leads to creative change. The components are referred to as the 4 Ps of creativity (Rhodes, 1961). An updated and more detailed representation of the system has been termed the Creative Change Model (Puccio, Mance, & Murdock, 2011).

Puccio, G. J., Mance, M., & Murdock, M. C. (2011). *Creative leadership: Skills that drive change* (2nd ed.). Thousand Oaks, CA: Sage Publications.
Rhodes, M. (1961). *An analysis of creativity*. The Phi Delta Kappan, 42(7), 305-310.

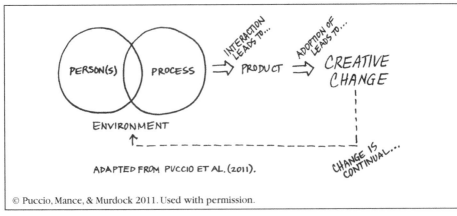

ADAPTED FROM PUCCIO ET AL. (2011).

46–47 POSITIVE ECOSYSTEMS

Based on the Creative Change Model and Mel Rhodes's original work (see notes for pages 48-49), the Creative Learning Ecosystems Model (Haydon, 2015) shows educators how creativity can be leveraged for deep, rigorous learning and student success. Each of the original 4 Ps of creativity is represented in education terms: *Persons:* teacher, student, and parent attitudes and outlooks; *Process:* curriculum and teaching methodologies; *Press (Environment):* classroom management practices and physical space; *Product:* ideas and knowledge applied (Haydon, 2015).

Haydon, K. P. (2015). What if we view our education system as an ecosystem? In Culpepper, M. K., & Burnett, C. (Eds.), *Big questions in creativity 2015.* Buffalo, NY: ICSC Press.

48–49 PEOPLE

Many researchers have found that, unfortunately, society tends to be biased against creative individuals (Csikszentmihalyi, 2013; Mackinnon, 1978). Some people are surprised to know that research has revealed that teachers "typically view the ideal student as compliant and conforming" (Beghetto, 2010, p. 454).

Beghetto, R. A. (2010). Creativity in the classroom. In Kaufman, J. C., & Sternberg, R. J., (Eds.), *The Cambridge handbook of creativity* (pp. 447-463). New York, NY: Cambridge University Press.

Csikszentmihalyi, M. (2013). *Creativity: The psychology of discovery and invention* (New ed.). New York, NY: Harper Perennial.

Mackinnon, D. W. (1978). *In search of human effectiveness: Identifying and developing creativity.* Buffalo, NY: Bearly Limited.

50–51 STRENGTHS MISLABELED

E. Paul Torrance first taught at a school for boys who had disciplinary issues. He realized that the special spark he noticed among the boys was creativity. Many of these boys went on to do great things later in life, but at school and at home their strengths were misunderstood and unsupported. A psychologist who worked in the fields of creativity and gifted education, Torrance had a quest to broaden the definition of giftedness to include creative people who were misunderstood or under-recognized as minorities (Cramond, 2013; Millar, 1995). Other scholars have also sought to expand the definition of intelligence beyond the traditional IQ test. Creativity is often a factor in these definitions. For example, Robert Sternberg's Triarchic Theory of Human Intelligence (1984, 1997) includes analytical intelligence, creative intelligence, and practical intelligence. More recently, Scott Barry Kaufman (2013) proposed the Theory of Personal Intelligence: "Intelligence is the dynamic interplay of engagement and abilities in pursuit of personal goals" (p. 302).

The list of creative traits and their negative interpretations on page 50 is influenced by Davis's (2004) work.

Cramond, B. (2013). The life and contributions of E. Paul Torrance. In E. Romey, (Ed.) *Finding John Galt: People, politics, and practice in gifted education* (25-31). Charlotte, NC: Information Age Publishing.

Davis, G. (2004). *Creativity is forever.* Dubuque, IA: Kendall-Hunt Publishing.

Kaufman, S. B. (2013). *Ungifted*. New York, NY: Basic Books.

Millar, G.W. (1995). E. Paul Torrance: The creativity man. Norwood, NJ: Ablex Publishing.

Sternberg, R. J. (1984). *Beyond IQ: A triarchic theory of human intelligence*. New York, NY: Cambridge University Press.

Sternberg, R. J. (1997). *Successful intelligence: How practical and creative intelligence determine success in life*. New York, NY: Plume.

52–53 IDEAS

Divergent thinking, or idea generation, has several sub-components: fluency, flexibility, originality, and elaboration. Fluency is the ability to come up with many ideas and alternatives, not just a few. Parnes (1961) was the first to prove through a research study that during brainstorming obvious ideas are voiced first, good ideas are voiced second, but the most novel ideas come out in the last third. In other words, the more ideas generated, the better the chance of a unique one.

Parnes, S. J. (1961). Effects of extended effort in creative problem solving. *Journal of Educational Psychology* (52),3,117-122.

54–55 EXPRESSION

It might sound counter-intuitive to consider that well-known creative people have consistent routines. This carves time and space for the expression of ideas. The main commonality among eminent people's routines is that each approach is highly individualized, tailored to that person's particular needs and preferences (Currey, 2014).

Currey, M. (2014). *Daily rituals: How artists work*. New York, NY: Alfred A. Knopf.

56–57 CARING FOR IDEAS

The simple act of making separate time for divergent (idea generation) and convergent (idea evaluation) thinking is a powerful tool to enhance and practice creativity. Alex Osborn, partner and "O" of New York ad agency BBDO, invented brainstorming after observing that in his firm, many good ideas didn't stand a chance from the beginning. He studied the way ideas were formed and proposed by teams within the organization, and came up with strategies to help increase the possibility that good ideas would come to fruition.

Osborn outlined four guidelines for effective ideation sessions: withhold judgment until later; welcome wild ideas; strive for a great quantity of ideas; and combine and build upon ideas (Osborn, 1953). With these guidelines, he cautioned that evaluation of ideas should be done after ideation. In his experience working with hundreds of brainstorming sessions, criticism or evaluation of ideas during divergent thinking shut down the sharing of ideas. The point of Osborn's work was to give those who were faced with the need to collaborate the tools to harness the contributions of each member of the team, and to minimize the potential of ideas being doomed before they could be fully vetted.

Osborn, A. F. (1953). *Applied imagination*. New York: NY: Charles Scribner's Sons.

58–59 JUDGING IDEAS

Convergent thinking is an evaluative process, when ideas are assessed and chosen. Isaksen & Treffinger (1985) proposed the following guidelines for convergent thinking: *Be affirmative.* Ask, "What's good about this idea?" *Be deliberate.* Give every idea a chance. *Check your objectives.* Always keep your goal in mind. *Improve ideas.* Be aware that some ideas might be in rough stages; make time to improve them. *Consider novelty.* Don't be turned off by truly unique ideas; consider how they might be workable.

Isaksen, S.G., & Treffinger, D.J. (1985). *Creative Problem Solving: The basic course.* Buffalo, NY: Bearly Limited.

60–61 COLLABORATION

Collaboration is a reality of life—at work, in a family, and at school— and can often be exhilarating. On the other hand, individual creativity is important as well. Osborn (1953) emphasized the need to ideate as an individual first, and then to collaborate, especially during convergence: "To insure maximum creativity in teamwork, each collaborator should take time out for solitary meditation. By working together, a pair is more likely to achieve the best in creative thinking" (p 146). His suggested divergent thinking climate of deferred judgment, informal play, and psychological freedom parallels the work of Ekvall (see notes for pages 64-65).

Osborn, A. F. (1953). *Applied imagination.* New York: NY: Charles Scribner's Sons.

62–63 PROCESS

Wallas (1926) was the first to depict creativity in stages: preparation, incubation, illumination, and verification. More recently, Puccio, Mance, and Murdock (2011) defined a series of seven steps in the deliberate Creative Problem Solving (CPS) process: assess the situation, explore the vision, formulate challenges, explore ideas, formulate solutions, explore acceptance, and formulate a plan (p. 73).

Puccio, G. J., Mance, M., & Murdock, M. (2011). *Creative leadership: Skills that drive change* (2nd ed.). Thousand Oaks, CA: Sage Publications.

Wallas, G. (1926). *The art of thought.* New York, NY: Harcourt, Brace & Company.

64–65 ENVIRONMENT

Göran Ekvall is known for his work identifying and measuring organizational climates that support creativity and innovation. He defined organizational climate as "recurrent patterns of behavior, attitudes, and feelings that characterize life in an organization" (Ekvall, 1999). The words in the photo on page 64 are the ten climate dimensions that impact creativity in organizations, and can be assessed using Ekvall's Situational Outlook Questionnaire (Isaksen, Lauer, & Ekvall, 1999). In summary, they relate to trust, respect, freedom, safety, support, and lack of negative pressure. Nine of the dimensions are positive influences on a climate supportive of creativity and change, but conflict (or emotional tensions) is an inhibitor.

Ekvall, G. (1999). Creative climate. In M. A. Runco & S. R. Pritzker (Eds.), *Encyclopedia of*

Creativity, Volume I, A-H. (pp. 403-412). San Diego, CA: Academic Press.
Isaksen, S. G., Lauer, K. J., & Ekvall, G. (1999). Situational Outlook Questionnaire: A measure of the climate for creativity and change. *Psychological Reports*, 85, 665-574.

66–67 OUTCOME

The outcome of the creative process is typically referred to as the "product." Creative products don't have to be physical; they can be also insights, solutions, and theories. In order to effect change, the outcomes (products) must be applied or implemented. This is what causes change, otherwise known as innovation (Puccio, Mance, Switalski, & Reali, 2012).

Susan Besemer spearheaded much of the early research on evaluating creative products. Her Creative Product Analysis Matrix assesses products along three dimensions: Novelty (How original are the concepts, processes, or materials used?); Resolution (How well did the product resolve the problem?); and Elaboration and Synthesis (Is the product stylized with refinement and elegance?) (Besemer & O'Quin, 1987; O'Quin & Besemer, 1989).

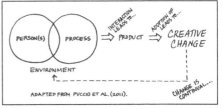

Besemer, S.P., & O'Quin, K. (1987). Creative product analysis: Testing a model by developing a judging instrument. In In S. G. Isaksen (Ed.), *Frontiers of creativity research*: Beyond the basics (pp. 341-357). Buffalo, NY: Bearly Limited.
O'Quin, K., & Besemer, S. P. (1989). The development, reliability, and validity of the revised creative product semantic scale. *Creativity Research Journal*, 2(4), 267-278.
Puccio, G. J., Mance, M., Switalski, L., & Reali, P. D. (2012). *Creativity rising: Creative thinking and creative problem solving in the 21st century*. Buffalo, NY: International Center for Studies in Creativity Press.

68–69 GOING BEYOND

Torrance wrote (1991), "The word 'beyonder' is not in the English dictionary, yet almost everyone seems to understand its meaning" (p. 69). Through his work, he identified the top ten most common Beyonder characteristics: 1). Delight in deep thinking. 2). Tolerance of mistakes. 3). Love of one's work. 4). Clear purpose. 5). Enjoying one's work. 6). Feeling comfortable as a minority of one. 7). Being different. 8). Not being well-rounded.* 9). Sense of mission. 10). Courage to be creative (Torrance, 1995, p. 152). Garnet Millar (2004) summed it up: "Being a Beyonder means doing your very best, going beyond where you have been before, and going beyond where others have gone" (p. 1).

* Here, Torrance meant that people should not be prevented from pursuing their interests due to pressure to be "good at everything."

Millar, G.W. (2004). *The making of a Beyonder*. Bensenville, IL: Scholastic Testing Service, Inc.
Torrance, E. P. (1991). The beyonders and their characteristics. *Creative Child and Adult Quarterly*, 16, 69-79.
Torrance, E.P. (1995). *Why fly?* Norwood, NJ: Ablex Publishing.

ABOUT THE AUTHORS

Kathryn Haydon is a keynote speaker and consultant to families, schools, and organizations. An innovative educator working to change the paradigm to one based on student strengths and creative thinking, she seeks to turn the fix-in mentality upside down by asking, "What lights up this child and how can we leverage it?" Kathryn co-authored *Discovering and Developing Talents in Spanish-Speaking Students* (Corwin, 2012), writes for publications on education and creativity, and is a regular contributor to *The Creativity Post*. She is also a published poet. As a former teacher, Kathryn founded Ignite Creative Learning Studio in 2009 and Sparkitivity in 2012 to engage "square peg" students, and to support the parents and educators who want them to succeed. She holds a Master of Science in Creativity, Creative Problem Solving, and Change Leadership from the International Center for Studies in Creativity at SUNY Buffalo State and a Bachelor of Arts from Northwestern University. Please visit at **sparkitivity.com**.

Jane Harvey is an insightful artist, designer, graphic recorder, and visual facilitator. She is a creativity expert valued for her openness, empathy, and humor, and her three decades of experience in design. As a former 'creative' in a Fortune 100 company, she saw that people's creativity is typically underused and undervalued in organizations. In addition to freelance design work, Jane encourages and facilitates individuals, businesses, and students toward creative thinking and innovation. She earned a Master of Science in Creativity, Creative Problem Solving, and Change Leadership from the International Center for Studies in Creativity at SUNY Buffalo State, and has a Bachelor of Fine Arts from Parsons School of Design. Please go to **visualtranslating.com** to learn more about Jane's recent work.

CPSIA information can be obtained at www.ICGtesting.com
Printed in the USA
BVOW10s0250150715

408635BV00007B/7/P